LEVEL
I

McMaster
English

Contents

Contents

01
Animal

1 Animal

Bees are very diligent. They fly around flowers. They collect some pollen from flowers. They make honey from it. They make their hive bigger and stronger together.

1. What is the main topic of the passage?

   a. Pollen from flowers

   b. Diligent bees

   c. Honey for bees

   d. Bee hives

2. What is the main idea of the passage?

   a. Bees fly around a person.

   b. Bees make honey.

   c. People do not like bees.

   d. Bees are diligent.

II

A. Underline the key word of the passage and write it.

Giraffes are the world's tallest land animals. They have long legs and long necks. Their long necks reach the top of the trees.

_____

_____

_____

B. Underline the topic sentence of the passage and write it.

Monkeys are very popular at the zoo. Many people enjoy seeing the monkeys. And they like to give the monkeys some bananas.

_____

_____

_____

Giant pandas are endangered animals.

They mainly live in southern and eastern China.

Their food is unusual. It's bamboo.

After 1920, people began

to cut bamboo trees. So giant pandas

lost their food. And people hunted them

to get some medicine and skins.

The number of giant pandas on Earth today is about a thousand.

1. **What is the main idea of the passage?**

    a. People hunted giant pandas.

    b. The giant pandas are endangered animals.

    c. People got some medicine from giant pandas.

    d. Giant pandas' food is unusual.

2. **What is true about the giant pandas?**

    a. They are safe.

    b. They mainly live in western China.

    c. They eat bamboo.

    d. They cut bamboo trees.

IV

Dolphins usually live in the ocean. But people can also find dolphins in some rivers. River dolphins are mammals. So, they have babies and feed their young with milk.

They have long beaks and sharp teeth. And they feed on small fish. Because they have poor eyesight, they cannot be trained for shows like sea dolphins.

1. What is the main topic of the passage?

   a. River dolphins

   b. Sea dolphins and river dolphins

   c. River dolphins' eyesight

   d. River dolphins' babies

2. How is a river dolphin different from a sea dolphin?

   a. It can swim faster.

   b. It is a mammal.

   c. It feeds its young with milk.

   d. It has poor eyesight.

Actual Mini *TOEFL*

Every bird lays eggs. Birds' eggs look weak, but they are, in fact, very strong. Because of its oval shape, the egg is not easily broken.

The birds try to find safe places for their eggs. So they usually make their nests somewhere out of sight. Some birds build their nest on the high roofs. Other birds make nests in dark caves. And many birds make their home in the holes.

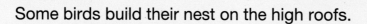

1. **What is the main idea of the passage?**

   a. Birds make their eggs strong.

   b. Birds' eggs are not easily broken.

   c. Birds make nest and lay eggs.

   d. Birds are very diligent.

2. **Why do some birds make nests in caves?**

    a. Because they can make the nests quickly.

    b. Because the caves are safe for the eggs.

    c. Because the caves are quiet.

    d. Because the caves are warm.

3. **What makes the egg strong?**

    a. Its shape

    b. Its colour

    c. Its size

    d. Its smell

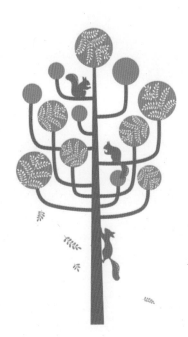

American Indian

02

2 American Indian

A. Underline the key words of the passage and write them.

American Indian's names are interesting.
They have special names. For example,
a baby's name may be "Crying Jumper,"
because she cries very wildly.

_____

_____

B. Underline the topic sentence of the passage and write it.

Indians enjoy music.
They like to sing and
dance. They play music
when they are happy or

sad. They have many kinds of musical instruments.

_____

_____

II

Read the following sentence and answer questions.

When Columbus found America, there were about 13 million people on the land. He believed that America was the India of Asia. So he called the native people Indians. Today, they are called American Indians.

American Indians lived by hunting or farming. And they had various cultures. But their cultures were destroyed after Europeans came to America.

1. What is the main topic of the passage?

   a. The war between Europeans and Indians

   b. American Indians' hunting

   c. The history of American Indians

Basic Reading

III

Indians hunted millions of buffalos. They hunted the buffalo in groups. And they used horses to catch more buffalos. Indians made clothes with buffalo skin. And they made brushes with buffalos' tails. They even ate buffalo meat. Buffalos gave everything to Indians. So buffalo hunting was essential to them.

1. What is the main idea of the passage?

   a. The buffalo is endangered.

   b. Indians used horses to hunt buffalos.

   c. Buffalo skin was very useful.

   d. Buffalo hunting was important to Indians.

2. Which of the following did the Indians not do with the buffalo?

   a. They rode buffalos.

   b. They ate buffalo meat.

   c. They made clothes.

   d. They made brushes.

Actual Mini *TOEFL*

When the English people came to America, they brought some wheat. But it didn't grow on the land. So Indians taught them how to grow corn and other vegetables.

Thanks to the Indians' help, they harvested corn at last. So they invited the Indians to celebrate. They also thanked the God for their first harvest on the new land. It was a special time of friendship between them. It was the first Thanksgiving in America.

1. **What is the main topic of the passage?**

   a. People from England

   b. Indians' first harvest

   c. The origin of Thanksgiving Day

   d. How to grow corn

2. How could English people grow corn in America?

   a. They learned from Indians.

   b. They learned for themselves.

   c. They read many books about corn.

   d. They learned from farmers in England.

3. What is not true about the first Thanksgiving?

   a. English people invited Indians to celebrate.

   b. English people thanked God for their first harvest.

   c. It was a time for friendship between Indians and English people.

   d. Indians fought English people.

03

Painting

3 Painting

A. Underline the key words of the passage and write them.

> There are many books on painting in the book store. Many of them are very helpful for beginners. But some are not very good, because they are too difficult to read.
>
> _____
>
> _____

B. Underline the topic sentence of the passage and write it.

> Painting is easy and simple. Start with a sketchbook, a pencil and some watercolors. Sketch anything interesting and paint with watercolors.
>
> _____
>
> _____

II

Read the passage and answer questions.

Claude Monet is a French painter. He was born in Paris, in 1840. He usually drew outdoor landscapes. He drew a picture only when lighting conditions were good.

From 1872 to 1878, Monet lived in a village on the Seine River. And there he painted his most famous works of Impressionism. In his final

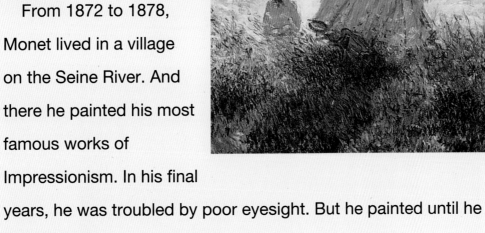

years, he was troubled by poor eyesight. But he painted until he died in 1926.

1. **What is the main topic of the passage?**

   a. A famous painter's life

   b. The places where Claude Monet lived

   c. Claude Monet's hobby

   d. Claude Monet and his friends

2. **When did he draw his most famous picture?**

   a. When he studied in Paris.

   b. In his final years

   c. Before he married.

   d. When he lived near the Seine River.

III

Read the following passage and answer questions.

One of the most famous museums in the world is the Louvre Museum in Paris. The Louvre was once a palace built for the king's of France. It was opened as a museum in 1793.

It has lots of famous collections. They are from various cultures. The collections are paintings, sculptures and prints. They are exhibited in seven departments.

1. What is the main topic of the passage?

   a. The biggest museum

   b. The history and collections of the Louvre

   c. A French building

   d. Famous collections

2. Which of the following is true about the Louvre Museum?

   a. It is a new building.

   b. It was once a palace.

   c. It exhibits only paintings.

   d. It was opened by a French king.

Actual Mini *TOEFL*

Materials of Chinese paintings are paint-brushes, ink and paper. They are important in Chinese paintings.

The Chinese paint-brush is similar to a watercolor paintbrush. But it has a finer tip. Ink was used in paintings for over two thousand years. When the ink cake is ground on the stone with water, ink is made. Chinese paintings may be done either on Chinese paper or on silk. Some papers are rough and others are smooth.

Read the following sentences and answer questions.

1. What is the main idea of the passage?

   a. Chinese paintings are interesting.

   b. There are many kinds of paintings.

   c. The materials are important in Chinese paintings.

   d. To choose materials is difficult.

2. What is not necessary to make ink for Chinese paintings?

   a. Ink bottle

   b. Ink cake

   c. Stone

   d. Water

3. What do people use for Chinese paintings instead of paper?

   a. Brush

   b. Silk

   c. Ink

   d. Stone

04
Movie

4 ▸ Movie

A. Underline the words that *he* refers to and write it.

When a film director makes a movie, he plays many roles. He changes the scripts, coaches acting and works together with the staff. Sometimes *he* acts in the movie.

_____

B. Underline the words that is closest in meaning to "movie" and write it.

My mother and I sometimes go to the movie theatre. But it is difficult to choose the *movie*, because I always want to watch an animation film.

_____

II

Read the passage and answer questions.

Watching a movie is a hobby for many people. But people like different kinds of movies. There are horror movies, romantic movies, animation movies and so on.

When people choose a movie, their reasons are also "_different_". Some people choose a movie because of an actor or an actress in "_it_". Others think that the story is more important than anything else.

1. The word "it" in the passage refers to

    a. a history   b. a movie

    c. an actor   d. an actress

2. The word "different" in the passage is opposite in meaning to

    a. difficult   b. easy

    c. same   d. various

III

From childhood, Steven Spielberg was interested in movies and he wanted to go to film school. But the school didn't _accept_ him.

He entered the university and studied English. But he didn't give up his dream. One day he found an old closet and turned _it_ into an office. He started his work as a director and finally he succeeded.

Read the passage and answer questions.

1. **The word "it" in the passage refers to**

   a. The university   b. His dream

   c. A closet   d. An office

2. **The word "accept" in the passage is closest in meaning to**

   a. give   b. admit

   c. make   d. pick

Actual Mini *TOEFL*

Shrek is an animation film. It has three main characters. They are Shrek, Donkey and Fiona.

Shrek is a big, green, ugly monster. He lives in his swamp "*by himself*". He enjoys taking mud showers, and eating forest insects. *His* friend Donkey likes to talk, sing and dance. His character is humorous and charming.

Princess Fiona is smart and tough. But she becomes short, fat and ugly in darkness.

1. **What is the main topic of the passage?**

    a. three friends

    b. animation movie

    c. characters in Shrek

    d. Prices Fiona

2. The word "His" in the passage refers to

    a. Shrek

    b. Monster

    c. Donkey

    d. Fiona

3. The words by "himself" in the passage is closest in meaning to

    a. alone

    b. lonely

    c. strongly

    d. sadly

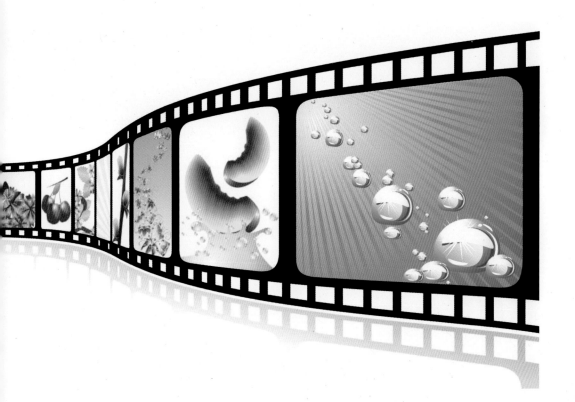

05

Transportation

5 Transportation

A. Underline the words that "them" refers to and write them.

We sometimes hear news about car accidents. Most of *them* are serious.
The people are hurt badly.
And the cars are smashed.

_____

B. Underline the words that is closest in meaning to "exercise" and write it.

Riding a bicycle is a good sport. It is safe and healthy. The *exercise* is also helpful for a clean environment, because it does not pollute the air.

_____

_____

II

Read the passage and answer questions.

People ride vehicles such as buses, motorcycles and cars. Many people go to work by car or bus. Police officers usually ride motorcycles.

But it is sometimes _dangerous_ to ride these vehicles. Especially driving _them_ fast may cause a serious accident. Therefore the people should drive carefully and wear a seat belt or a helmet.

1. The word "them" in the passage refers to

   a. police officers   b. vehicles

   c. accident   d. people

2. The word "dangerous" in the passage is closest in meaning to

   a. interesting   b. boring

   c. tired   d. unsafe

III

A long time ago, people rode horses. Today, we usually travel by automobiles.

The first automobile was invented in France in 1769. *It* was very big and slow. And it *moved* by steam from boiling water. Later inventors made gasoline-powered automobiles. They were safer and lighter than the steam-powered cars.

Read the passage and answer questions.

1. **The word "it" in the passage refers to**

   a. horses

   b. France

   c. the first automobile

   d. gasoline-powered automobile

2. The word "moved" in the passage is closest in meaning to

    a. went

    b. made

    c. invented

    d. used

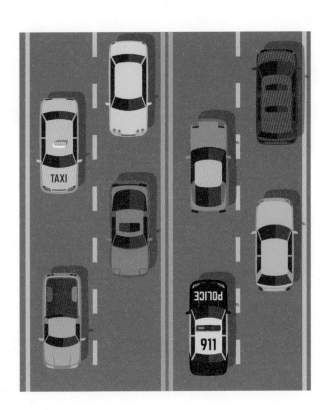

Actual Mini *TOEFL*

There are many traffic signs along the road. The signs control traffic and *guide* a vehicle or a person. They also warn of dangerous road.

The traffic signs are made of metal or plastic. And they have simple words or pictures. Each of "*them*" has a different meaning. For example, the picture of a sliding car warns that the road is slippery. And the word "STOP" says that you have to stop the car.

1. What is the main topic of the passage?

    a. the words on the traffic signs

    b. the pictures on the traffic signs

    c. the traffic signs

    d. warning of danger on the road

2. The word "them" in the passage refers to

    a. roads

    b. words or pictures

    c. metal or plastic

    d. vehicles

3. The word "guide" in the passage is closest in meaning to

    a. control

    b. warn

    c. lead

    d. stop

06

Plants

6 Plants

I

A. Arrange the sentences in order.

a. They make it from the air, water and soil.

b. Plants make their own food.

c. They also need sunlight.

_____

_____

B. Choose the sentence that will come next and write it.

Roots get water from soil.

a. They grow bigger and taller.

b. All plants need water.

c. The water travels in the plants.

_____

II

Read the passage and answer questions.

There are many kinds of plants. Grasses, bushes and trees are all plants. (A) All plants have roots, stems, leaves and flowers.(B)

The flowers become fruits. (C) The seeds grow with air, water and sunlight. (D) They will become new plants and their flowers will bloom. Then they will give their fruits and seeds back to nature.

1. The following sentence can be added to the passage.

    The fruits have seeds in them.

    Where would it best fit in the passage?

2. What is not kind of plant?

    a. Tree   b. Sunlight

    c. Bush   d. Grass

III

We can eat most plants.
(A) We eat the roots of plants.
Some of these are carrots
and potatoes. (B) They
include cabbage and lettuce.
(C) We enjoy eating the fruit of plants.
(D) We even eat flowers such as broccoli. They are too many to
count. Actually, we eat every part of a plant.

Read the passage and answer questions.

1. The following sentence can be added to the passage.

   We also eat leaves.

   Where would it best fit in the passage?

2. **What is true about cabbage?**

   a. We can eat their roots.

   b. We can eat their leaves.

   c. We can eat their fruit.

   d. We cannot eat cabbages.

Actual Mini *TOEFL*

Scientists try to make new vegetables. (A) For example, they have made purple carrots and orange cucumbers.

(B) The new vegetables look different for a reason. (C) The vitamins make new colours. (D) Vegetables are **good** for health. These new vegetables are even better. They give people more energy. And they can help fight diseases.

1. The following sentence can be added to the passage.

   It is because of extra vitamins.

   Where would it best fit in the passage?

2. The word "good" in the passage is closest in meaning to

    a. carefully

    b. heavy

    c. harmful

    d. helpful

3. How do the new vegetables help people?

   a. They are colourful.

   b. They give more energy.

   c. They make new colours.

   d. They help people grow taller.

07

Cultures

7 Cultures

I

A. Arrange the sentences in order.

a. They draw a funny face on the pumpkin.

b. Finally, they put a candle in it.

c. Next, they cut out the pumpkin.

d. People make Jack-O-lanterns on Halloween.

_____

B. Choose the sentence that will come next and write it.

The Opera House gives the feeling of a ship.

a. It's roof is white and looks like sails.

b. It is in Sydney.

c. People sing and put on plays.

_____

II

Read the passage and answer questions.

The Sphinx is a famous building in Egypt. (A) It has a people's head a lion's body. (B) No one knows why the Sphinx was built. (C) They are huge and triangle-shaped. They are in a hot, dry desert. (D) It is mysterious how ancient people could build them. They did not have any modern equipment.

1. The following sentence can be added to the passage.

    Behind the Sphinx, there are pyramids.

    Where would it best fit in the passage?

2. **What do pyramids look like?**

    a. They look like trees.   b. They look like lions.

    c. They have a people's head.   d. It looks like a triangle.

III

Cave paintings are found in many places around the world. Through cave paintings, we can learn about the lives and the cultures of the ancient.

Ancient people painted pictures of their common lives. (A) They hunted animals for food. So they drew many animals. (B) Some of the animals in cave paintings still live on Earth. (C) They are horses and lions. (D) The mammoth is among them.

Read the passage and answer questions.

1. The following sentence can be added to the passage.

   Some are not alive in the world today.

   Where would it best fit in the passage?

2. Why did ancient people draw animals in their caves?

   a. Because they liked animals.

   b. Because they hunted animals.

   c. Because they were scared of animals.

   d. Because they could not see many animals.

Actual Mini TOEFL

(A) Birthday parties began in Europe a long time ago. (B) People had birthday parties to protect them from harm.

(C) Friends and family brought food, wishes and gifts. (D) The origin of the birthday cake came from the Greeks. They made round cakes and put candles on *them*.

The round shape means a long life. Today, we celebrate our birthday parties with gifts and round cakes.

1. What is the main topic of the passage?

   a. The origin of the birthday party

   b. The origin of the Greeks

   c. The origin of cakes

   d. The origin of gifts

2. The following sentence can be added to the passage.

   They thought gifts could protect them.

   Where would it best fit in the passage?

3. The word "them" in the passage refers to

   a. the Greeks

   b. people

   c. cakes

   d. candles

08
Music

8 Music

I

A. Arrange the sentences in order.

a. So he composed many Symphonies.

b. He showed unusual talent for music from his childhood.

c. His fifth Symphony is the most famous.

d. Beethoven was born in 1770.

_____

B. Choose the sentence that will come next and write it.

Some children practice the violin everyday.

a. Their parents buy them as an instrument.

b. They want to be a great violinist.

c. They have many kinds of instruments.

_____

Read the passage and answer questions.

Four kinds of stringed instruments are played in an orchestra. They are violins, violas, cellos and double basses. They have a similar shape, but their sizes are different. Violins are the smallest and double basses are the biggest.

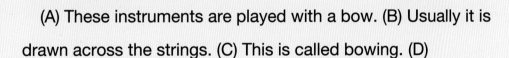

(A) These instruments are played with a bow. (B) Usually it is drawn across the strings. (C) This is called bowing. (D)

1. The following sentence can be added to the passage.

   A bow is a long thin stick.

   Where would it best fit in the passage?

2. What is not true about the stringed instruments?

   a. They have different sizes.　　b. Their shapes are similar.

   c. Violas are the biggest.　　d. They are played with a bow.

Ⅲ

Flutes are wind instruments. They have been made of wood. But most of them are now made of metal or silver.

(A) To play the flute, first we hold it sideways to our mouth. (B) Then we put our mouth near the holes at one end of the flute. (C) While we blow, we press the keys on the flute with fingers.

Read the passage and answer questions.

1. The following sentence can be added to the passage.

   And we blow over the hole.

   Where would it best fit in the passage?

2. Today what materials are needed to make most flute?

   a. string

   b. leather

   c. glass

   d. metal or silver

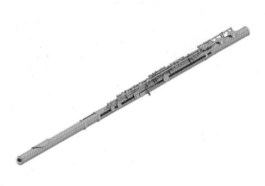

Actual Mini *TOEFL*

(A) Mozart was already a great musician when he was a child. (B) He composed his first opera when he was twelve. (C) He could compose music anytime. (D) He (wrote) music while talking to friends, swimming, or having meals.

Young Mozart traveled to many countries around Europe and played music. And he met famous musicians like Schubert and learned many kinds of music. Travel had an influence on his world of music.

1. What is the main topic of the passage?

    a. Mozart's travel

    b. Many famous musician

    c. Mozart's opera

    d. Mozart's early life with music

2. The following sentence can be added to the passage.

    He wrote his first short piece of music when he was five.

    Where would it best fit in the passage?

3. The word "wrote" in the passage is closest in meaning to

    a. composed

    b. learned

    c. played

    d. had

09
Literature

9 Literature

I

A. What can be inferred from the sentence? Circle it.

The Harry Potter books are one of the best-selling series for children.

a. Many children read Harry Potter.

b. The Harry Potter series is expensive.

B. Read the following paragraph and draw O if the following statements can be inferred and draw X if they cannot.

Aesop wrote many stories. Animals are the main characters in his stories. A fox or a wolf comes up very often in his stories. His stories give us wisdom.

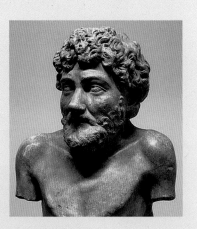

a. Aesop is a writer.

b. Aesop lived with animals.

c. We can learn good lessons from Aesop's stories.

II

Read the passage and answer questions.

A father had three sons. They quarrelled every day. The father was worried about it.

One day the father asked his sons to bring some sticks. Then he ordered each of them to break the bundle of sticks in pieces. No son could break them. Then he gave each son a stick and ordered him to break it. All the sons could break it. He taught them a lesson with the sticks.

1. Which of the following can be inferred from the passage?

   a. His sons learned that they should not quarrel with each other.

   b. The father did not like his sons.

   c. The father and his sons were very poor.

   d. His sons were too weak to break the sticks.

2. What did the father ask his sons to bring?

   a. tree   b. sticks

   c. friends   d. a lesson

III

A folktale is a traditional story told among people. It is not written down exactly. And its author is usually unknown. It's spoken from person to person. People add or change the story when they tell it to others.

You might hear a folktale from your mother or grandmother. Then you can tell it to your friends.

Read the passage and answer questions.

1. It can be inferred from the passage that

    a. only women like folktales.

    b. children wrote down folktale.

    c. a folktale has many variations.

    d. everyone likes to make new folktales.

2. According to the passage, folktales are usually

    a. spoken by people

    b. written by authors

    c. changed by children

    d. boring

Actual Mini *TOEFL*

Before you start to read a book, read the title first and read the introduction or summary. And think about the author's purposes and points. Then quickly look over heading and subheading and don't miss any graphics, charts or maps.

While you are reading a book, ask as many questions as possible. Why is he doing this? What would I do if I were the man? And try to answer *them*. You can learn more by doing so.

1. **What is the main topic of the passage?**

    a. how to choose a book

    b. how to read many books

    c. how to ask questions

    d. how to read a book

2. **It can be inferred from the passage that**

    a. Asking questions is a good reading skill.

    b. It is good to read only the summary.

    c. It is important to read many books.

    d. Some people enjoy reading.

3. **The word "them" in the passage refers to**

    a. books

    b. questions

    c. the man

    d. you and he

10

Pollution

10 Pollution

I

A. What can be inferred from the sentence? Circle it.

Cars are the main cause of air pollution.

a. Before cars were invented, the air was not very polluted.

b. More cars are necessary in the city.

B. Read the following paragraph and draw O if the following statements can be inferred and draw X if they cannot.

To save the polluted earth, use paper and plastic bags over and over again. Or buy a cloth bag and use it whenever you shop. Give your old clothes to someone else.

a. Reusing can reduce pollution.

b. A cloth bag is expensive.

c. A cloth bag can be used over and over.

II

Read the passage and answer questions.

Every day on Earth, people throw out countless tons of trash. The trash is from homes and businesses. It includes food scraps, paper, bottles, boxes, and cans, and even furniture, computers, and refrigerators.

It's important for homes and businesses to recycle and reuse. This can reduce the amount of trash. It can help protect the environment.

1. **Which of the following can be inferred from the passage?**

   a. Cans are not trash.

   b. Bottles cannot be reused.

   c. Factories throw out trash every day.

   d. The environment will become more polluted unless we recycle.

2. **Homes and businesses can recycle everything except**

   a. bottles   b. paper

   c. furniture   d. the environment

III

Many countries try hard to recycle waste. They build some factories and change waste to energy. The factories change waste into fuel. This fuel is used for making electricity. They provide electricity to homes and buildings in the city.

A city in Florida recycles one million tons of waste a year. If the waste is used for making energy, it is not waste any more.

Read the passage and answer questions.

1. It can be inferred from the passage that energy made

    a. cannot be used in hospitals

    b. is expensive

    c. is useful in homes

    d. is sometimes dangerous

2. What do many countries build to recycle waste?

    a. cities

    b. factories

    c. homes and buildings

    d. many countries

Actual Mini *TOEFL*

It is natural for the night to be dark. But the night sky is now bright. A special *kind* of pollution changed the night sky. It is light pollution. It has come from street light, cars and trucks. Lights from stores and office buildings shine in the sky.

(A) Because of light pollution, astronomers cannot study stars in the sky. (B) people cannot find their favorite stars anymore. (C) This is not only happenings in the cities.

1. The word "kind" in the passage is closest in meaning to

    a. food

    b. type

    c. bad

    d. reason

2. What can be inferred about office buildings

    a. Some people work there at night.

    b. They are a main cause of light pollution.

    c. They are usually very tall.

    d. They are brighter than moon.

3. The following sentence can be added to the passage

    Even in the countryside, people cannot see stars clearly.

    Where would it best fit in the passage?

11

American History

11 American History

A. Underline the words that "one" refers to and write it.

Samuel Johnson wrote the first English dictionary in 1755. In America, Noah Webster wrote the most *famous* one in 1828. It has been updated many times.

_____

B. Underline the word that is closest in meaning to "president" and write it.

Abraham Lincoln was the sixteenth *president* of America. He was a good leader and is still respected by many Americans.

_____

II

Read the passage and answer questions.

After the war was over, America won independence from Britain. People wanted to build a new *nation* and they needed a president.

During the war, many people admired George Washington. They thought *he* would rule over their country fairly. So he was elected as the first president of America. And Americans named the national capital after Washington.

1. The word "he" in the passage refers to

   a. war

   b. George Washington

   c. People

   d. Britain

2. The word "nation" in the passage is closest in meaning to

   a. city   b. farm

   c. country   d. town

III

Read the passage and answer questions.

The American flag is called "Stars and Stripes." A star on the flag means a state of the nation. *It* had only thirteen stars in 1777. As time *passed*, some stars were added for new states.

After Hawaii became the fiftieth state in 1959, it had fifty stars. And the flag became the official flag of the United States.

1. **The word "It" in the passage refers to**

    a. American flag

    b. star

    c. stripe

    d. state

2. **The word "passed" in the passage is closest in meaning to**

    a. had   b. added

    c. went by   d. needed

Actual Mini *TOEFL*

Thousands of people immigrated to America in the late 19th century. Most of them came from southern and eastern Europe.

American people didn't like the immigrants. *They* thought that the newcomers took their jobs. Moreover, the immigrants' religion was different from Americans'. So they could not live in harmony.

Finally America made a *law* to limit immigration. Because of this law much fewer people came into America.

Read the passage and answer questions.

1. **What is the main topic of the passage?**

    a. The history of the American immigration

    b. The history of American law

    c. The number of immigrants into America

    d. The immigrants' religion

2. The word "They" in the passage refers to

   a. immigrants

   b. American people

   c. jobs

   d. newcomers

3. The word "law" in the passage is closest in meaning to

    a. way

    b. note

    c. book

    d. rule

12
Human Body

12 Human Body

A. What can be inferred from the sentence? Circle it and fill in the blank.

The human body is special and mysterious.

a. The human hand is special.

b. A dog does not have
   a body.

_____

B. Read the paragraph and draw O if the following statements can be inferred and draw X if they cannot.

A person's brain controls all of his action. Each part of the body senses information and send it to the brain. The brain orders each body part to respond properly.

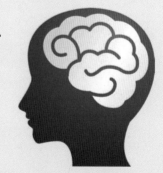

a. Without the brain, a person cannot move. _____

b. The nose sends information to the brain. _____

c. A bigger brain makes a person smarter. _____

II

Read the passage and answer questions.

The ear is an important organ of the human body. It sends sound waves to the brain.

It is made up of three parts. They are the outer ear, the middle ear, and the inner ear.

Ears are easily hurt. Therefore you should take good care of them. Be careful during swimming or washing hair. Don't listen to music that is too loud.

1. **Which of the following can be inferred from the passage?**

   a. Humans will die without ears.

   b. Some people have three ears.

   c. Very loud music can hurt the ears.

   d. To have healthy ears, we should swim.

2. **How many parts does an ear have?**

   a. One   b. Two

   c. Three   d. Four

III

Read the passage and answer questions.

The tongue is essential in speaking. The tongue moves in the mouth when a person speaks.

The tongue is also important in tasting. It senses sweet, salty, sour, and bitter tastes. If a person eats some chocolate, it will sense a sweet taste. If a person takes some medicine, it will sense a bitter taste.

1. **It can be inferred from the passage that**

    a. the tongue is fast.

    b. sugar tastes sweet.

    c. without the tongue, we can't speak.

    d. the tongue makes medicine bitter.

2. **The tongue can taste all of the following EXCEPT**

    a. sweetness   b. saltiness

    c. sourness   d. heat

Actual Mini **TOEFL**

The human body consists of many parts. They help you keep *strong*. Some parts help in digestion. They are the mouth, stomach, the small and large intestines. When you eat food, they move to digest the food.

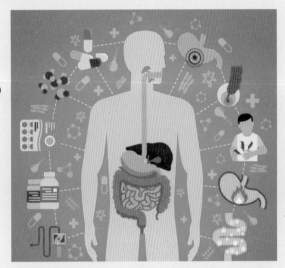

Let's take an example. If you eat some broccoli, the stomach begins to break down the broccoli. The softened broccoli moves into the small intestine. Vitamins, water and fiber from the broccoli are absorbed into the body.

Read the passage and answer questions.

1. **What is the main topic of the passage?**

   a. The human digestion system

   b. Eating broccoli

   c. Stomachache

   d. The mysterious human body

2. **Which of the following can be inferred from the passage?**

a. Broccoli doesn't have any water.

b. Small intestines are the most important part of the human body.

c. Broccoli is broken down easily.

d. The stomach helps in digestion.

3. The word "strong" in the passage is closest in meaning to

   a. weak

   b. healthy

   c. thin

   d. tall

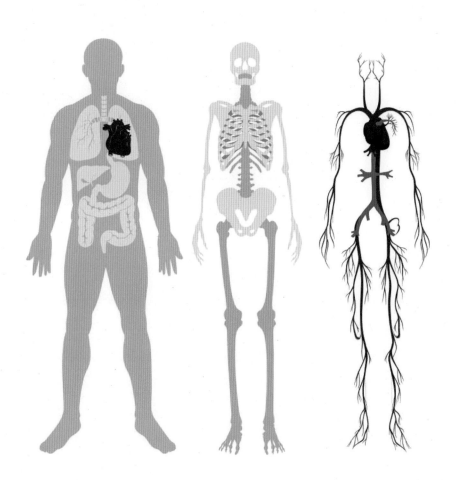

신봉수

고려대학교, Temple University [문학박사, 영어교수법(TESOL) 전공]

위덕대학교 영문과 교수 역임
위덕대학교 입학, 학생처장 역임

Senior Researcher & Visiting Professor
at Bilingual Research Centre of McMaster University (Canada)

저서: 영어교육입문 (서울: 박영사)
　　　영어교육의 이론과 실제 (위덕대학교 출판부)

McMaster English _ Basic Reading

초판1쇄 인쇄 2019년 5월 10일
초판1쇄 발행 2019년 5월 15일

편저자　　신 봉 수
펴낸이　　임 순 재

펴낸곳　　(주)한올출판사
등 록　　제11-403호
주 소　　서울시 마포구 모래내로 83(성산동, 한올빌딩 3층)
전 화　　(02)376-4298(대표)
팩 스　　(02)302-8073
홈페이지　www.hanol.co.kr
e-메일　　hanol@hanol.co.kr

ISBN 979-11-5685-771-6